Gay is natural

Gay is natural

How are you really doing ?
Are you enjoying your weekend ?
I'm sorry for if the screen is not that good
I will have to save up money to buy a new phone I think

(the video is called : the Nasty bit. you can watch it on youtube)

I have just finished working
It is Saturday
it is the 12th day in a row
I hope you don't mind that I lay down
 as I'm working more, I will need to rest more
 I'm walking
 I'm walking like every day ,my legs need to rest
I have prepared the cup of coffee
I've rolled a few tobaccos
you can get a cup of coffee too

I am not sharing my progress with you to to brag
or and I'm not thinking like uh look how great I am
 I just share it to help you and inspire you
because my message
my core message is and will be
 if I can do it so can you

because if a guy with a mental disability can work 7 days a week
then so can you
you can do it
absolutely

this is not a video or book that I should make it
should also not be online
so I will
I will warn you
if you can't laugh at yourself
if you can't laugh at your own shortcomings
and your own mistakes and the stupid things you do
 if you can't laugh at other people's shortcomings
and stupid stuff they do
 then you should not watch this video or read this booklet

so do you
do you ever wake up and you really have to go pee
 like really bad
and you just can't hold it and instead of going down to the toilet
you

you just go to the bathroom and you pee in the sink

you ever pee while you are taking a shower in the shower

have you ever been taking a shit and you wipe your ass
 and you're it's a long shit
you're a long time in there and you wipe your ass
and you wipe again and again and again and again
and then you flush and you flood the toilet

have you ever taken a shit and you're you're like tired and unaware
and you don´t shower
you do wipe but you don't wipe good enough
and then you're on the bus or the train going somewhere
 then it starts smelling like shit, and you're just unaware that it is your ass stinking

have you ever drank so much alcohol that
that you became sick and you throw up
but you're too tired and too ill to clean it up and you just go to bed
and the next day the sink is full vomit from it and it stinks
and then you clean it
and that evening you get drunk again
you just don't learn the lesson

well I'm glad that's a thing of the past
I'm sober for more than 50 days
and I will stay sober for the rest of my life

let me take a sip of coffee
do you drink coffee after 3:00 in the afternoon ?
you shouldn't because the cafeine
cafeine that's in it works for 6 hours and it will prevent you from falling asleep

do you drink black tea or green tea because you think it's healthy in the evenings
well it has theine in it which is the same as caffeine and it will prevent you from falling asleep

so you should drink teas like mint or Camonmille
 they don't have theine in them and they're much better

 I also don't drink coffee after 3:00 or 3:30 in the afternoon
so this will be my last cup
 or maybe after this one another one
and that would be the last one

you been fucking ,but you couldn't come ?
that's sucks ass

 have you ever ordered an escort and she was sucking your dick

but because of the nerves you couldn't come
 it sucks ass

 if you ever ordered an escort, a really beautiful one
because you think
 well don't have a girl
girl friend
not fucking for a long time it's not healthy
so I'll do it this way
 I'll pay and get get some get some fucking going on
and then you drink too much and you're fucking and you can't come because of the booze

Have you ever ordered an escort and paid extra
and you fuck her ,and you came on her face ?
well I did

have you ever ordered the escort and you paid extra so you can fuck her in the ass ?
well I did
and that's uh legal here in the Netherlands by the way
it's a whole industry

 it's uh it's a bit dirty and nasty for women to know about you
 so that's why this video and booklet is not for women

but those were my sexual fantasies
and I got to live them
 I got to experience them
and when I die
 I'm going out with a smile on my face

no unfulfilled desires
not a life of quiet desperation
but a good life
 I lived
I did the things I wanted to do
I fulfilled my desires
I worked
 I contributed
I loved
 I cried
I felt sad
 I felt happy
I gave
 I helped out
 I achieved some goals and now I'm achieving more goals
I'm not going to have regrets

have you ever fallen in love with a girl

and then you message her on Facebook
you send your sweetest messages
you send the joke
you send a poem
you ask about her day
you get a book of jokes, to find a good joke to make her laugh

and then she just blocks you

 and you're are stubborn and persistent
and you keep messaging her on another social media, on LinkedIn
and then you get blocked again

and you're stubborn like a jackass ,like I am
and then you start messaging her on Instagram
and you sing her a song
and you translate the song to her
and you ask her about her day
and you send hugs and kisses
and you don't know where she lives
you don't know the address
but you know the address of her work,
 so you send presents
 you send a mug
you send a Valentine's card
you sent not one chocolate bar but seven
you send books
you send another mug with her, how do you call it ?
 pet name on it

and then you get a letter
which says you should not be stalking her
and if you continue ,she will report you to the police

so how about that ?
all the things I have mentioned , I have done
yeah

you must probably be thinking
man you are really good like making an ass out of yourself
but who cares ?
four or five people will watch this video , (and read this book)
my sister will say to me man what the fuck are you doing ?
remove the video !
you should not be talking about those things

but why not let us
let us have some fun

right

I've made a lot of other videos
I've talked about serious topics
Let us laugh about my mess
about my fuckups
about my shortcomings
to make it easier for you to cope with your own shortcomings

well it was not like that I met her online
and I would be sending messages and gifts
we actually had worked together
we were co-workers at at this restaurant where I would work
many years ago
but she just never talked to me
she never said anything nice
only that intimidating letter
and the message which was also saying the same thing

 it was when I was drinking
and you should not drink because it
you should not drink alcohol
because it will make you very indifferent
it will make you not care
you will say and do things that you would not normally do
and they would create problems for you
so do whatever you can to avoid it
but drink liters of tea ,like I do
 and water, it's the best

so I thought well that's online
you know
 it would be best if I would meet her in person
that's always better
and then I would
I would very very soon
very rapidly learn how she really thinks and feels about me
 so if I would go to where she lives
 and I would work there, selling my greeting cars door to door
and I knock on her door …
I would soon find out what she really thinks
 if she slams the door in my face or curses me or something
 that that tells me enough
or it could turn out positive
and we would have a conversation
 right
so because I did not know what her address
I was curious and wanting to find out

so I know a guy who knows a guy
who knows a guy,
 right
who knows more guys
and I paid so that they would hack the municipality
how do you say it ?
the government
 and find the address for me
so that I could go and uh work in her neighborhood
and knock on her door
and talk to her
right
I well
 I'm I'm like stupid like that ,right

uh so but I I actually got kind of scammed
because he and they didn't deliver the address to me
and then I became tough on the guy
 I told him that if he
I have paided
 if he doesn't deliver
 that's scamming people
he should not be doing that
and I I said I will block you until you deliver
 right

so you can be tough and good at the same time
right

but that's one thing
and I only did two other things
 in the past two decades that I'm on my best behavior
and I will continue to be on my best behavior for the rest of my life..
 I like this life
 it is peaceful
without problems
 without me causing problems for myself
but I did that
to have some fun right

and well it's the things we do for love right

there are only two other things
 I got fined because I walked through a red light
it's it's no big deal
and I got fined because I was walking besides the track of the train
 one time I was working in another Village
 and I missed the train

and I thought and it was weekend and they only go once an hour
it was cold
so I thought what should I do?
 I can wait for an hour and be bored here
or I can start walking towards home
I did not know the route to my home
 but I knew if I would walk besides the track of the train
 it would be a straight line to to my city and to my home
so that's what I did
and then someone saw me and they called the police
and they came
and I told them the well that's not the law
then they told me well it is
look here at this sign
 I didn't see the sign
so I got another fine

but that's only three things in two decades
it's not the it's not a big deal

all so what more should we talk about ?
those are my fuckups
and my nasty things
 and they should not be online
but let us have some fun

how about
how about finding your balls?
 or if you're a woman, finding your ovaries ?
holding them
and Having the courage
 to be brutally honest to people
like I am doing right now
and to be brutally honest with yourself
and laugh at your short cumings
and your fuckups
like I did

I said online
I'm always honest
but
but it's true
it's not like uh just words

I have a business
I sell door to door
 I must be
other wise people will see through it

or they would find out
and they would lose trust
and then nobody would buy from me
and what
what uh should I do then ?
close the business down
 I can't do that
I'm committed to my business
 it's a lifetime thing
 selling the greeting cards
 and writing more books and selling the books

maybe you're wondering what do I think about gay people ?
well not much…
 I can say this
 if a boy is born and he grows up and around 16, 17 years old
maybe
 maybe at this era
 it's way sooner
he starts to like girls and they make him horny and he fucks with them
and he falls in love with them
 that is natural …

and if another boy is born and he grows up
and at that same age he finds out that he likes other boys
and they make him horny
 and he falls in love with them
 then that's natural too….

 so uh what do I think about it ?
I think the same as the pope does
he said ´´who am I to judge ?´´

 I think the lesbians and the gays
 that they have a function in life
there are kids without without parents
who are orphans
and if you have kids from divorced parents
or kids from who have lost their parents
and who are orphans
in their puberty they will become problematic

 my parents have divorced
 and in my puberty I became problematic

 but these orphans
 they miss parents
 they miss the love and attention

sure they get some in an orphanage
 but it's still not the same
and then these uh lesbians and these gays
 they will they will adopt such a kid
and give him parents
 and give him love
and give him the attention that it needs
 to become a good person
 and make something out of himself
and out of his life

so I think that's their function in the world
and because of that
they are not a mistake
but they are
they are designed by God for a purpose
right

so I have complete peace with them
and two lesbians playing with each other
 that's just hot
 that's hot for every man
 right

so I am not having any strong opinions
or judgments or whatever about these people
they don't bother me
what they do in their bedroom, they keep to themselves
 they are not trying to involve me
they are not trying to involve you
they're not bothering you with it
they keep it private
so why should you be bothered by them
it is to live and to let live
right

live the peaceful life
 all right
 what more should we talk about ?
well my sister will not like this
 and she will not like the following
because
because it's too personal
but I can share it with you
 if you keep it a secret
if you keep this video a secret

she has two kids

her husband is Turkish
she's Bosnian
the kids are half Turkish, half Bosnian
 they are beautiful
 they are smart
 they give me joy and love

my niece made a bracelet for me
 I'm wearing it every day
 they have made drawings for me
 I have them at the kitchen door ,
so that I see them every day …
but unfortunately
 her husband left her
 he's living at his mother's house
and sometimes
 sometimes times she gives them money
and sometimes he doesn't
and my sister can't work
because the kids are too young
she's on a government income
but that's only enough for survival
kids need more money
she has a car
 it's uh expenses
 right
 taxes
 gas
insurance
and when I visited them yesterday
and I bought them two bags of groceries
to help out
 it is one of my duties ,to help them
 like Andrew Tate says ''to provide and protect''
 right

 but when I was waiting for the bus
 at the train station
 I was thinking about this
so what if he what if he pays this month
 and doesn't pay the next month?
 and then pays again and then not pays again
 and it continues like that …

 or what if he
 what if he don't
  what if she doesn't go to court
  and force him to pay alimony ?

or what if they do
and and he says
that all this money is going into living expenses
and and he won't pay

like was the case with my father and my mother

or what if like with the relationship that my mother had
with this guy
he would only pay groceries and her health insurance
but that's not the half of living expenses
and if you are living together
you should pay at least half of of the living expenses
right

so what if he pays on a regular basis
but he pays like this guy
and it's just not enough
what then ?

so Grant Cardone said once that when his father died
he hoped very much that one of his uncles would
would step up
and take him under their wing

and now I'm thinking about this
and history could repeat itself
so it's a bit scary
and I became really uncomfortable
and I was thinking about this
and I must uh
I must Step Up as an uncle
I must work more
I must work harder
I must give more
so that they are supported and provided
regardless of uh what her ex-husband does
it is my duty anyway

some would say that this is God's way of of forcing you to to rise
to a higher level of success
that might be true
when he makes things uncomfortable for you
you have to get better and rise to a new level of success

so how did I cope with it ?
well I am

I am Rising today
I thought about what I had previously done
 you know the promotion
buy two get one for free
so today I would sell my packages of greeting cards
and one package for 5 euro
 and I would say
three three packages for €10
 right

 so they buy two and they get one for free
and it it will help me to to make more cash and profit
 well I'm actually visiting the same amount of people
so it's good
 it's a good promotion
and I have I have plenty of greeting cards in stock
 so I can easily do it
and two people took the deal
and I've earned more today than yesterday
which is good

what more should we talk about ?
so I obviously have more work to do
 I also have to help my mother
I have
so like last year I gave money to my mother and my sister
every month
 and this year I must do the same but
 but give them more
because everything has gotten more expensive
all the companies have raised their prices
so there is a bigger need for more cash
 and it's my duty to provide
 and I will

so how did I cope with this chick ?
that has sent me that letter to tell me to fuck off
 I was sad
and I was a little bit angry
I was…
 just kept thinking
why did she not say nothing nice to me
 right
I've sent her the sweetest and the best messages that I could think of
 but there was after months
 there was absolutely no reciprocity
 only those two three messages telling me to fuck off
 so I decided that I must move on

because life always goes on
and that I should do the same
and I've actually done what andrew tate teaches
he says like

'' if you're sad or depressed or angry you should channel that into productivity into work and use that energy it's unlimited energy sadness is energy to achieve more and to become better ''

so that's what I did
I wrote more books
I started working 7 days a week
I went more often to the gym
I trained harder
and I thought
 I thought well I'm going to just become better and more successful
and achieve more
and so that one day uh
she will feel like uh like that she made a mistake
by not giving me a chance

it is the best way to cope with this kind of stuff

so now I'm like
 I stumbled upon a woman online
and she made me laugh
 and she's also very attractive
and I started to feel things
and I wrote her a poem
actually two
 and I will continue to give her attention
and to say kind things…
 but if she decides that I'm a weirdo
that I'm a creep
 that I should go get fucked
and back off
well guess what ?
that will only Aid me
it will only help me
 I would do the same like I did the last time
I use the energy to work more
to write more
 to produce more
to achieve more
and I will win either way

so there you go baby
the beautiful American

oh I hope this inspires you to overcome things
and to use them to become better
 and achieve more
 it's the best way to handle it
 it's the best way to cope with it all
right

 I think I've told you all the nasty stuff from my life
 I hope I have taught you more understanding about people who fall in love with the same
sex it is the wise King Solomon from the old ages that said
you know
 In all you're getting, get understanding

so now you understand them better
and their purpose
you can live more peaceful with them
and not be judgmental at all
I hope that helped

and I hope that you now know how you should cope with
and overcome heartache and other bad shit in life
that will happen to you
 it is just meant for you to become better
 to rise
to achieve more
to channel that energy into productivity

and one of the lessons is also
 if a guy with a mental disability
who sees people and eyes and faces and and shit
that doesn't exist
for which I have medicine now
 but it still occasionally happens

 if he can write 185 books
and work his way into the top of writers
 if he can work 7even days a week in this fucking cold
then so can you
 you absolutely can do it
 all right
 I hope I've inspired you
I hope you have gotten some value from this
 and I also hope that you were able to laugh at my shit

if you got some value from this
 please share it with other people
 all right then

thank you for your time and attention
until next time
bye-bye
Chiao chiao

About the author :

Jasmin Hajro grew up in Bosnia untill the war started,

the family moved a couple of times within the country

when the fighting and shooting came to close.

Eventually Jasmin, his mother and sister were able to flee the country

to the Netherlands. Father had to stay there and fight as a soldier in the war.

The family lived temporarely in a few asylum centers for refugees

and finally got a house in the city Doetinchem.

Father got shot in the war, almost died, and was also able to leave the country.

The family was reunited for a short while, and soon Jasmin´s parents divorced.

The kids went to school, father and mother worked. Father remarried.

Jasmin got a diploma from school, he was good in languages.

He had a difficult puberty, where used drugs and drank a lot of alcohol,

he also broke the law a few times. After using too many drugs, he got into a coma

and barely survived. After that, he completely left that life and those people behind him.

He worked at several jobs. He started in 2007 as a dishwasher at Landal greenparcs

he worked his way up to cook and got lifetime employment.

After collapsing a few times, he also stopped drinking beer.

Unfortunately he started hallucinating at work,

soon he couldn´t sleep, focus or work.

He lost his work...

He started a investment company in december 2012

he failed. In 2015 while he couldn´t find a job,

he got sales training from his sister

and he received packages of greeting cards, and started selling them in his

neighbourhood. After a while ,he started designing his own unique greeting cards.

He was writing in journals for many years, and in 2017 he wrote and selfpublished his
first book : Build your fortune.

He always kept on writing new books,

by now he has written more than 60 books

he also translates his Dutch books into English.

He has been diagnosed with his mental disability,

he now has 2 medicines, one against hallucinating and the other to be able to sleep.

He has gotten a income from the government to pay for living expenses.

His company is called Hajro International B.V.

he sells his packages of greeting cards, door to door.

His company helps people with disabilities and with low incomes, by giving them money

It also donates to a few good charities.

Jasmin lives in Zelhem by himself and his 3 cats, Sjakie, Jinx and Jingle.

Jasmin is a nice and generous person. He visits his mother, his sister and her 2 kids
every week. He gives away more than 100 of his ebooks at smashwords for free.

His journey continues to become a better salesman, writer, entrepreneur

and to help a lot of people with his books , and his teachings on youtube.

Please be supportive, buy more of his books

Learn from his video´s and livestreams

And share his work with your friends, family

and the booklovers that you know.

Thank you very much.

Imagine if you could read a book that would not only touch your heart but also change your perspective on life. A book written by an author who not only has incredible talent, but is also an inspiring go-getter in the face of challenges. Meet author Jasmin Hajro, an exceptionally talented writer who is not held back by his disability, but who turns his limitation into strength.

Jasmin Hajro's books take you on an emotional journey full of profound insights, powerful stories and incredible life lessons. Not only does he overcome the obstacles he faces, but he also shows you that there are no limits to what you can achieve if you are determined and believe in your own abilities.

What makes Jasmin Hajro's books really special is the sincere, moving way he tells his stories. He knows better than anyone how to touch you with his words and make you feel

deep down what it means to be human. His ability to convey complex emotions in an accessible way is truly extraordinary.

But there's more than that. By buying Jasmin Hajro's books you not only support a talented author, but you also contribute to creating an inclusive society. You show that limitations do not diminish someone's value or potential, but rather that we should value and learn from the unique perspectives and experiences of others.

Be inspired by the resilience, perseverance and courage of Jasmin Hajro. Buy his books not only for yourself, but also as a valuable gift for your loved ones. Discover the power of his words and let them encourage you to dream bigger, feel deeper and be stronger.

So don't hesitate, pick up a book by Jasmin Hajro and get ready for an unforgettable reading experience. Enrich your life with his thoughts, emotions and insights. Discover the beauty of being human through the eyes of an exceptional author. Every book you buy makes a difference not only in your world, but in the world of someone determined to prove that limitations are only a temporary hindrance on the road to greatness.

For Jasmin´s entire lifestory, grab a copy of Life and business of Jasmin Hajro

Visit Jasmin and his company at www.hajro.es

or the international www.hajro.co

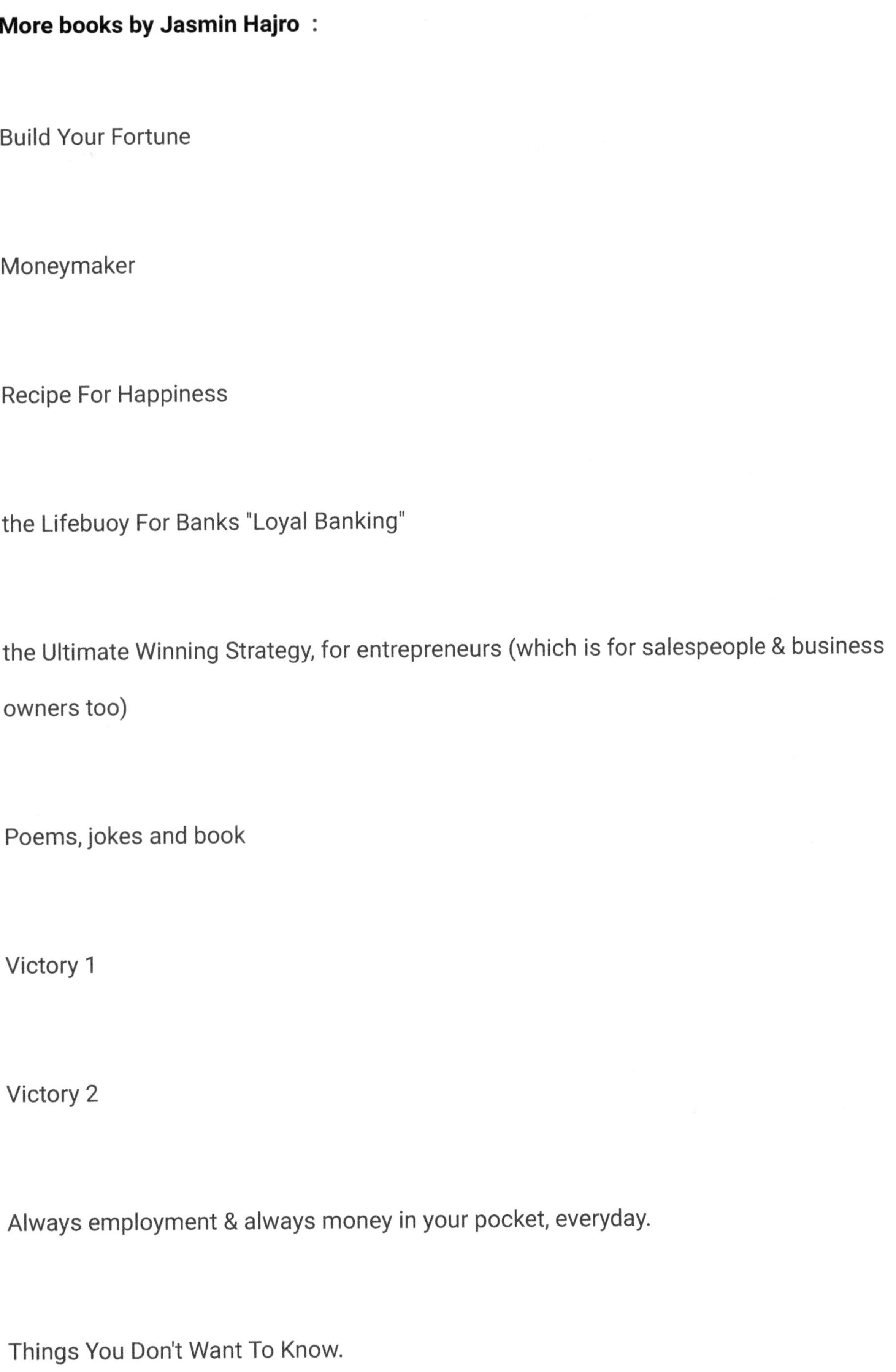

More books by Jasmin Hajro :

Build Your Fortune

Moneymaker

Recipe For Happiness

the Lifebuoy For Banks "Loyal Banking"

the Ultimate Winning Strategy, for entrepreneurs (which is for salespeople & business

owners too)

Poems, jokes and book

Victory 1

Victory 2

Always employment & always money in your pocket, everyday.

Things You Don't Want To Know.

Challenges in having your own business, in real life.

how to Grow your money & Build a good retirement in 2 hours per month, for moms, dads, career women and busy people .

Overcoming tough times.

Secrets of writing and selling books.

Double your profits.

Double your profits, extended.

Triumph 1 (boxset)

Triumph 2 (boxset)

Victorious series (boxset)

Through the crisis

Last 10 years

Unknown millionaire

This is the real secret to success, forget mindset, shiny objects and the law of attraction

Zucchini, dagen van een schrijver

Suiker maakt je dik (Sugar makes you fat)

P.a.w.

Geluk in een ongeluk (Good luck in bad luck)

Nederland is super (the Netherlands is great)

How they keep you poor

Tired ?

How to make money online

Life and business of Jasmin Hajro

Fix your shit

You shine bright

Daily prayers for muslims

The adventures of Skippy (childrens book)

Productivity crash course

Gay is natural

____

Recommended books :

Recipe for happiness

Best buy, how not to get scammed

the Ultimate Winning Strategy, 2nd edition

P.a.w.

Faster way to riches and success

This is the real secret to success

Life and business of Jasmin Hajro

Peace

Recommended children´s books :

(to give as a gift or to read to your kids or grandkids, fun stories and valuable lessons)

the Adventures of Skippy

Saving pennies with Mimy

____

Enjoy more than 100 free Ebooks

Be kind and give Jasmin a helping hand...by sharing the app with people you know who enjoy reading books.

Thank you.

Dutch titles :

Bouw jouw fortuin

Moneymaker

Recept voor geluk

de Reddingsboei voor banken, loyaal bankieren

de Ultieme Winnende Strategie

Gedichten, grapjes en boek

Victorie

Victorie 2

Altijd werk en altijd geld op zak, iedere dag

Dingen die je Niet wil weten

Victorious serie

Work to shine serie

De kunst van goed advies geven

Coole jongen

Jouw eigen bedrijf starten en succesvol maken, in de keiharde realiteit, waar het niemand interesseert

Te persoonlijk, handgeschreven

Te persoonlijk, handgeschreven 2

Moeilijke tijden overwinnen

Beveiliging en bescherming van jouw zaken en jouw bedrijf

Victorie 3

De pen die je 100.000,- euro oplevert

Tieten, hoe schrijf ik een boek ?

Voor jou

Grote ballen

Vrede

Legacy serie (2 delen)

Mijn verslaving overwinnen

Gewoon doorgaan

Ondernemen met hersenschade

Entrepreneurship cursus

Dirty money

de Ultieme winnende strategie, voor schrijvers

My story

De geheimen van goede sex, 30 boeken schrijven, een levenspartner vinden en geld verdienen zittend op je reet

Het geheim van afvallen, het geheim van goed leven en mijn schrijfsels

In loving memory

Ziba

Actie als strategie

Running out of time

Hajro story en catalogus

Voor Saartje

Exposium

Rahima en Idriz

Suiker maakt je dik

Dagelijkse gebeden voor moslims

Geluk in een ongeluk

De avonturen van Ixi

40 Praktische manieren om te stoppen met je zorgen te maken

Opgelicht door een goed doel ?

Kinder bedtijd, voorlees verhalen voor het slapen gaan

De magie van inspiratie, verhalen die levens veranderen

Nederland is super

Zucchini, dagen van een schrijver

Vrede

Wijsheid voor je betere leven

Kinderen leren van dieren (kinderboek)

Introducing Jasmin Hajro's books: discover, share and become a fan!

Are you an avid reader with an insatiable appetite for compelling stories? Search no further! Get ready to dive into a world of imagination and emotions as you journey with Jasmin Hajro's and her captivating books. Moreover, you can now enjoy her collection for free, share them with your friends and acquaintances and ultimately become a devoted fan.

Jasmin Hajros is an incredibly talented author who has created a wide range of literary gems. Her books span a variety of genres, from romance and mystery to fantasy and science fiction. Whatever your preference, you're sure to find a book that will keep you browsing long into the night.

But that is not everything! In addition to her exceptional storytelling, Jasmin Hajro's unique ability to dig deep into the human psyche, delve into complex themes and capture the essence of human nature. Her characters are relatable, their struggles gripping and their triumphs truly inspiring.

Now imagine having the opportunity to share these literary treasures with your friends and loved ones. By accessing Jasmin Hajros's books for free, you can not only enrich your own reading experience, but also introduce others to the magic of her stories. Spark conversations, stir emotions, and create timeless memories together as you explore the captivating worlds Jasmin has created.

In fact, if you delve into her books, you'll undoubtedly become a devoted fan. Jasmin Hajro's unique storytelling style, rich character development and masterful plot twists will captivate your heart and leave you wanting more. Join a community of passionate readers who share the same enthusiasm for her work and participate in discussions, fan theories and exclusive content.

So don't wait any longer. Unleash your imagination, experience the joy of sharing stories with friends and become a devoted fan of Jasmin Hajro's books. With her freely available collection you have the perfect opportunity to explore new worlds, enrich your reading journey and unleash your imagination.

Get started today and witness the magic of Jasmin Hajros' stories firsthand!

Do you want to enjoy the brilliant works of author Jasmin Hajro? Now you can download, read and even gift free ebooks to your friends and family!

Jasmin Hajro is a talented writer who tells stories that capture your heart, stimulate your imagination and make you think. With his compelling stories, interesting characters and profound messages, he can surprise, inspire and motivate you.

This is a unique opportunity to access his valuable bibliography, which will entertain and enrich you. Whether it's suspenseful fiction, enchanting novels, or insightful self-help books, Jasmin Hajro's works are sure to leave an impression on you.

By downloading these free ebooks, you can not only enjoy great literature, but also surprise your friends and family with a gift that has lasting value. Send them a story that you think will inspire them, move them or broaden their horizons. In this way you not only share the joy of reading, but you also contribute to the personal growth of others.

This opportunity is too good to pass up. So what are you waiting for? Visit our website and discover a world of stories that will captivate you. Download Jasmin Hajro's e-books, read them yourself or give them as a gift to your loved ones. Spread the joy of reading and experience the power of words.

Don't miss this great opportunity to discover the talented author Jasmin Hajro and inspire others. Download the free ebooks today and be enchanted by his masterpieces!

Get more than 100 books of Jasmin for free

download the free Ebook app at : https://eu.jotform.com/app/232615553904355

Excerpt book Best buy, how not to get scammed

the ultimate guide on how to live healthier, wealthier and happier

while protecting yourself from being scammed

and loosing money, heart disappointments and time..

Multiple books in one bundle covering

happiness, wealthbuilding, living happier, increasing sales and profits..

covering trading, cryptocurrency, investing in stocks and private equity,

books, courses, MLM's, gurus, business & investing & earnings opportunities which are scams,

plus a resources to stay aware and away from scams not covered.

Get this guide now and save yourself money ,time, disappointment

and robbery of your peace of mind.

How did I get through 2020

year of corona....

Recipe for Happiness

How to reduce stress and live happy

The Ultimate Winning Strategy

how do successful companies earn more and win

Last 10 years

It's personal...and business

quitting drugs and alcohol

starting to build a better life

then getting mental problems

and ending on the street

failing with my first company and

then starting a new company

asking for help and getting rejected multiple times

untill finally I get the help that I need

because my sister and a friend went with me

my last 10 years with a lot of tough times

maybe my experiences can help you

If you want to live happier and wealthier, why don't you try it

Introducing "Peace" by Jasmin Hajro - a groundbreaking exploration into the existence of universal intelligence, commonly referred to as God. In this thought-provoking book, Hajro skillfully presents a logical and rational perspective on the age-old question of the divine, offering readers a refreshing and insightful understanding of the universal intelligence that underpins our existence.

Through the pages of "Peace," readers will embark on a journey of enlightenment, delving into the very fabric of the universe to uncover the logical explanation for the existence of universal intelligence. Hajro's compelling insights and meticulous reasoning will challenge conventional beliefs and inspire a deeper contemplation of the mysteries of life and the cosmos.

With clarity and precision, "Peace" invites readers to explore the interconnectedness of all things and contemplate the profound implications of universal intelligence on our lives. Whether you are a seeker of spiritual truth, a philosopher pondering life's deepest questions, or simply someone with a curious mind, this book offers a transformative perspective that transcends traditional dogma and encourages a more profound understanding of our place in the universe.

Engaging, thought-provoking, and intellectually stimulating, "Peace" is a must-read for anyone seeking a logical and coherent explanation for the existence of the universal intelligence, shedding new light on age-old questions and providing a foundation for personal growth, spiritual awakening, and a deeper sense of peace and understanding.

Join the countless individuals who have been enlightened and inspired by "Peace" by Jasmin Hajro. Embrace a new understanding of the universal intelligence and embark on a journey toward greater peace, knowledge, and enlightenment.

Excerpt book Faster way to riches and success

What other books forget to tell you ,and how to join the top 10%

To become successful and rich while you are still young.

Has goal setting not worked?

What is the real difference between success and failure?

And between the top 10% and the other 90%

How can you shorten the path to getting rich

How to be a success every day

This booklet gives you the answers that you have been looking for...

If you are paying the price for success every day, you are a success and becoming a greater success

This is what other books fail at telling you about getting success and riches

Review :

Shobana Gomes

4.0 out of 5 stars

Faster Way to Riches and Success

Reviewed in the United States on February 25, 2023

This book generally talks about the practicality of doing the right groundwork in order that the business expands and excels. Mr. Hajro gives his views and personal experiences, citing business experts and their models to success.

In Mr. Hajro, the desire to inspire and lead people by example is prevalent just as he outlines in this book. This quote sums up his actionable thoughts well: all successful people are action-oriented, they're always moving - Jasmin Hajro